EPITAPHS TO REMEMBER

EPITAPHS TO REMEMBER

Remarkable Inscriptions from New England Gravestones

by JANET GREENE

Including many Epitaphs transcribed and collected by Thomas C. Mann

(Formerly published as *Over Their Dead Bodies*)

Illustrated by George Daly
Foreword by Castle Freeman

Alan C. Hood & Company, Inc.
BRATTLEBORO, VERMONT

Epitaphs to Remember

(Originally published as *Over Their Dead Bodies* by
The Stephen Greene Press)

Copyright © 1962 by The Stephen Greene Press

Manufactured in the United States of America

Published by Alan C. Hood & Company, Inc.
Brattleboro, Vermont 05301

Library of Congress Cataloging-in-Publication Data

Greene, Janet C.

Epitaphs to remember : remarkable inscriptions from New England
  gravestones / by Janet Greene ; including many epitaphs
  transcribed and collected by Thomas C. Mann ; illustrated by
  George Daly ; foreword by Castle Freeman.
      p.   cm.
  Previously published as: Over their dead bodies / Thomas C.
Mann and Janet Greene, 1962.
  Includes index.
    1. Epitaphs—New England.   I. Mann, Thomas C. (Thomas
Clifford), b. 1890.   II. Mann, Thomas C. (Thomas Clifford),
  b. 1890. Over their dead bodies.   III. Title.
PN6291.G74 1993
929.5—dc20   93-32624
                                                                   CIP

ISBN 0-911469-10-9

10 9 8 7 6 5 4 3 2

ACKNOWLEDGMENTS

OF THE MANY published books and articles collected as cross-references, by far and away the most scholarly for its range is *Stories on Stone, A Book of American Epitaphs* by the Rev. Charles W. Wallis (New York, 1954). Valuable for their photographs of gravestones are Harriette Merrifield Forbes's *Gravestones of Early New England and the Men Who Made Them, 1653-1800* (Boston, 1927), Robert E. Pike's *Granite Laughter and Marble Tears* (Brattleboro, Vt., 1938) and the fine and thorough articles by Ernest Caulfield, M.D., on gravestone carvers of Connecticut in the *Bulletins* of the Connecticut Historical Society.

All researchers including the authors are indebted to the statewide old cemetery associations in their area, and to local cemetery groups, all of whom are working hard to preserve their graveyards and, in many cases, to publish records of the stones in their burying grounds.

For their help in recommending or providing background material the authors are especially grateful to Professor Richard M. Judd of Marlboro College; to Professor Leon W. Dean of the University of Vermont, president of both the Vermont Old Cemetery Association and the Vermont Folklore Society, for guidance in winnowing the authentic from the unlikely; to the staffs of the Boston Athenaeum and the Brattleboro Free Library; to Mrs. Pierson Fogg and Mrs. Thomas Storrow of the Stonington (Conn.) Free Library and the Stonington Historical Society, respectively; to Miss Clara Follette, Secretary of the Vermont Historical Society; to R. L. Dothard for his comments on the changing styles of lettering on old and new gravestones; to Dante Bai Rossi for information about production of modern memorials, and to such knowledgeable authors and friends as Richard Sanders Allen, Walter

ACKNOWLEDGMENTS

Hard Sr, Walter Hard Jr, Ralph Nading Hill, Florence Thompson Howe, R. L. Kolvoord, Nell M. Kull, Gladys E. Neiburg, Frank H. Teagle and Herbert Willard.

The authors are beholden to Obelena Greenleaf Cutting for typing, Diana Gould for patient and enlightened help in organizing and to Eleanor Bartlett Lowe and Debbie Coleman for their aid in checking the final manuscript.

And for their assistance in collecting epitaphs or hunting down elusive facts we thank Antonio Abbiati, Harry Anderson, George S. Bevis, Lillian Bragg, Theda Brigham, Norman Broadridge, Alice Bullock, William Callahan, Blanche Carpenter, Mary Casey, Madeleine Chase, Fred Cheever, Marjorie Coller, René Columbus, Donald Corliss, Mildred Dufresne, Lloyd Ellison, Marguerite Evans, Alvin Gamage, Edith Gassett, Caryl George, Polly Hicks, Doris Hopkins, John Huden, Jessie Hulet, Oscar Johnson, Pauline Knapp, Thomas LaFlam, Jane W. Lloyd, Beatrice Loiselle, Lillian Mattoon, Jane Moyes, Louise Wilbour Nelson, Maolyn Palmer, Ann Perry, Robert Pierce, Eone Powers, Merrill E. Redfield, Rena B. Reed, Monica Remillard, R. Hubert Rogers, Mazie Rose, W. A. Ross, Ruth Sherman, Myrtle Small, G. Milan Smith, Robert Smith, Leslie Stearns, Charles Stevens, Margaret Steward, Elmer Stoddard, Fred Thomas, Elizabeth Thompson, Helen G. Upton, James Watson, Henry Weaver and R. Wentworth.   T.C.M. & J.G.

CONTENTS

FOREWORD

To THIS READER, at least, Janet Greene's elegant collection of New England epitaphs has much of the charm of a novel. Not a new novel. Not a novel in which the author with great travail forges in the smithy of his soul the uncreated conscience of his race (while we watch); but rather a novel from an older tradition. The inscriptions here, or more exactly the men, women, and children whose lives they were written to commemorate, seem to me to make up the kind of long, rich, comforting story in which we are given a social world complete. By my quick count, 305 characters figure in this slender volume, as well as 4 wars, 6 drownings, 5 murders, and any number of lesser catastrophes. Fielding or one of the great Russians would have needed a thousand pages to tell such a story, Greene manages the job handily in ninety-nine.

The memorials themselves come from some two hundred cemeteries in the six New England states, but in the book they form a single whole and the people whose graves they mark form a kind of community. Consider how rich and various a community it is. Here are all ages, all trades. Here are rich and poor, high and low, the best and the worst. Here is a petty thief whose luck ran out in a little town at the top of Vermont (No. 198), and here is the President of Yale (No. 25). Slaves, soldiers, divines, (*many* divines), Indians, sea captains, judges, schoolteachers, blacksmiths, inventors, crowd these pages. They fill them with passion, with indignation, with self-satisfaction. They fill them–oddly enough, given the single undoubted qualification for ownership of an epitaph–with life.

More remarkable than the conditions of the many characters arrayed in this book are their ideas. Again as in the literature of a simpler time, the real people whose inscriptions we find here are by their epitaphs reduced to what we may as well call their meanings. In particular, our cast includes every kind of religious believer, from the more or less conventional, to the mildly peculiar (No. 17: *Who*, exactly, are the second class of extremists Mr. Park declares have beset the world since ye fall of Adam?), to the cheerfully agnostic (No. 171, 174), to the tiresomely atheist (No. 204). In addition, we find a colorful parade of eccentricities, *idées fixes*, and hobby horses: spirit-knockers, rationalists, Copperheads, Perfectionists, flat-earthers, Masons, anti-Masons, and herbal practitioners.

Despite the oddities and the shocking dissolutions of so many of their protagonists, however, the story these inscriptions have to tell is very much the story of ordinary human relationships, and in particular it is the story of marriages, of husbands and wives devoted and otherwise (No. 156) and their children. It is rich in love, and in the nature of things it is rich in sadness, but best of all it is rich in wit. The epitaphs delight in turning the most violent, painful experience into doggerel, wisecracks, and one-liners. It is their humor that gives the memorials their curious charm, especially for readers like ourselves whose time has done so much to prolong and safeguard life that we may begin to take death too seriously. Perhaps we should look to that idea for the moral of the story the epitaphs embody. (It's an old-style story, remember; it may have a moral.) For if we can learn not to take death too seriously, surely we can learn the same for life. That is a useful lesson, and it's one that is enforced over and over again in the pages that follow, though to me nowhere more eloquently than on the stone of Mary Lefavour, of Topsfield, Massachusetts (No. 70):

> *Reader pass on and ne'er waste you time,*
> *On bad biography and bitter rhyme*
> *For what I am this cumb'rous clay insures,*
> *And what I was is no affair of yours.*

Castle Freeman, Jr.
Newfane, Vermont
June 1993

PREFACE

THERE IS NOTHING morbid in the hobby of collecting epitaphs from cemeteries—unless it is in searching old graveyards for the chance of a laugh at a startling inscription. For being startled is the reason why 20th-century visitors may think the statements on gravestones are funny. Conditioned as we are by the fairly new taste for muted and above all discreet markers, it is easy to be jolted into regarding testaments which violate modern reserve as irresistibly quaint or humorous. It is perfectly logical that the anthologies harping on America's or New England's comic epitaphs have all been published after the epitaph was on its way out as a personal record of fact or belief.

Being hauled up short by an unexpected sentiment over a grave is a natural reaction but it needn't be a permanent one. The collection on which this book is based started as the result of wanting to know more about a colonial housewife whose capture by Indians was the basis of an historical novel. Jemima Howe? She was a Sartwell before she married Howe. No—before that she was married to Phipps. But what of the third husband . . .?

All that was needed was to follow the practice of other researchers: we went to the graveyard where she is buried. There were the dates and the spouses and the descendants and, since it is an old one, what was important in their time about the people involved—what they lived by and what they died for—carved into the stones. And any initial surprise at the stunning frankness of Jemima's and neighboring inscriptions was erased by gratitude for the rich chronicle they offered of contemporary ideas and events. This affection for the epitaph as a personal testament has increased over the years, and makes us wish heartily that records like these had not gone out of fashion.

Reticence is the criterion for tombstones today. The

quirks and the pivots in the lives of those lying beneath them are seldom mentioned and the fact of dying, except through the date of decease, next to never.

The trend is easy to follow back in Yankee burying grounds. It first appeared early in the 19th century when epitaphs began being written expressly to soothe the bereaved. Until then the carvings had warned of the inevitability of death and decay and had promised mercy on Judgment Day only as a reward for pious exercises or the revelation of God while on earth; and there were commendations of the qualities and services of the dead in the favored literary styles of Britain, and less sophisticated accounts of tragedy or fortune. Blunt indeed; but they reveal the tough-mindedness of people who lived in fear of their Lord but who did not, in the language of space-age anxiety, run scared.

Then soon after 1800 the number of admonitions and personal histories decreased: for death rendered less grim and life less intense somehow made bereavement less painful; there came more and more inscriptions about eternal peace and reunions in heaven. The final development has been to omit even these muffled cries of the heart.

Yet though today᾽ markers are reverent in their dignity, it is the stones which bear messages of personality that appeal to strangers. Wandering with a companion through an old cemetery is neither a depressing nor a frivolous pastime, but is pleasant in the strict meaning of gratifying the mind and the senses. We brush chalk across letters to make them more legible; we read, and we see ourselves in these people now gone and recognize the day-by-day ingredients of our continuity.

With several exceptions the epitaphs in this book are vouched for as authentic, either because they were transcribed by the authors or because they were furnished by serious collectors. The exceptions are ones that have circulated by public fancy without being bolstered by dates and family names and verified locations; they are so noted and are included for what they are worth as grave-yard folklore.

There is no attempt to reproduce the lettering of inscriptions, though general trends in design are shown in the illustrations and outstanding innovations are mentioned as they occur.

The epitaphs are presented chronologically in four sections—but many of them overlap the strict dates of the movements that prompted them. The first section covers pioneer and colonial life through 1775, and the second spans the next forty years of national shaking-down and a new religious revival. The third division treats from 1816 through the Civil War, the great period of social ferment and humanitarianism. The last section, from 1871 to the present, indicates the decline of the Yankee epitaph as a declaration of belief and a record of social change.

Each section will have its own introduction in general terms and only enough to set the scene, for it would be a shame to explain away all the flavor of these explicit last words. The people who wrote them certainly didn't.

I. *Through 1775*

THE MOST POWERFUL intellectual forces in New England from the mid-1600's to the Declaration of Independence were the concepts that all men were created equal before God and that therefore church government, and hence by corollary civil government, should be by the consent of the governed.

The inspiration for rebellion against Puritan authority was the first Great Awakening, which began early in the 18th century to preach that salvation from hell's fire could be assured only through the inward revelation of God. However such free-thinking must be read between the lines of epitaphs; its political expression occurs just before the break with Great Britain. Otherwise the inscriptions reflect established doctrines holding that obedience to the requirements of piety, church-going, thrift and hard work would do much to guarantee heaven—

Pioneer and Colonial Life

subject to predestination or the awful Judgment of God.

Meanwhile the Puritans were supporting public education and the growing interest in science: Cotton Mather hunted witches but he was also among the first to advocate inoculation against smallpox; later Thomas Clap refused to sanction anything but rigid conformity to Puritanism but he fostered the study of mathematics and the physical sciences at Yale College. And as the result of experiments by a Quaker named Benjamin Franklin it was decided that lightning was a phenomenon of nature, not a sign of divine wrath, and therefore it was not impious to equip Boston churches with lightning rods.

The stones also testify to epidemics and the rigors of frontier life and bear out Franklin's comment that marriages in America generally were more early than those in Europe, and that widowhoods were brief.

1

1. WILLIAM PADDY, 1658, age 58, Boston, Mass.:

> Hear sleaps that
> Blesed one whoes lief
> God help vs all to live
> That so when tiem shall be
> That we this world mvst leve
> We ever may be happy
> With blesed William Paddy.

2. PLYMOUTH, MASS.:

> Here ended ye Pilgrimage of
> John Howland who died Feby 23d 1672-3
> Aged above 80 yeares. He married
> Elizabeth daur of John Tilley who
> came with him in ye shipp Mayflower
> Decr. 1620. From them are
> descended numerous posterity.

3. BOSTON, MASS.:

> Capt Thomas Lake
> Aged 61 Yeeres
> An Eminently Faithfull Servant
> Of God & One of a Publick Spirit
> Was Perfidiously Slain By
> ye Indians at Kennibeck
> August ye 14th 1676
> & Here Interred The 13 Of
> March Following

◆§ 4. WATERTOWN, MASS.:

Here lyes ye precious dust of

Thomas Bailey:	A most desirable neighbor,
A painfull preacher,	A pleasant companion,
An eminent liver,	A common good,
A tender husband,	A cheerful doer,
A careful father,	A patient sufferer,
A brother for adversity,	Lived much in little
A faithful friend,	time.

A good copy for all survivors.

AEtat. 35

He slept in Jesus ye 21st of Jany 1688

◆§ 5. ALSO IN Watertown, Mass.:

Lydia Bailey

Pious Lydia made and given by God
as a most meet help to John Bailey
Minister of ye Gospell
Good Betimes—Best at Last
Lived by Faith—Dyed in Grace
Went off singing—Left us weeping
Walk'd with God till translated in
ye 39 year of her age. April ye 16, 1691

Read her Epitaph
In Prov. xxxi. 10, 11, 12, 28, 30, 31.

◆§ 6. REBECCA NURSE, hanged in Salem in 1692, age 71, and later exonerated in the general revulsion against the persecution, whose relatively modern monument in Danvers, Mass., says in part:

Accused of witchcraft
She declared
'I am innocent and God will
clear my innocency.'
Once acquitted yet falsely
condemned she suffered
death July 19, 1692,
her Christian character even
then fully attested by forty
of her neighbors.

7. NEWBERRY, MASS.:

Mr Henry Sewall (sent by
Mr Henry Sewall, his father,
in ye ship Elsabeth & Dorcas
Capt. Watts Commander)
Arrived at Boston 1634:
Winterd at Jpswich helped
Begin this plantation, 1635
Furnishing English servants
neat cattel, & provisions.
Married Mrs. Jane Dummer,
March ye 25. 1646.
Died May, ye 16. 1700.
aetat. 86. His fruitfull
Vine, being thus disjoind,
Fell to ye ground January
ye 13. Following; aetat. 74.
Psal. 27 10

4

◄§ 8. DEERFIELD, MASS.:

The Dead of
1704

The Grave of
48 Men, Women and
Children, Victims
of the French and
Indian Raid on
Deerfield,
February 29, 1704

◄§ 9. CAMBRIDGE, MASS.:

Here lyes ye body
of Mrs Joanna
Winship Aged 62
years who departed
this life November
ye 19th 1707

This good school dame
No longer school must keep
Which giues us cause
For childrens sake to weep.

◄§ 10. NEWPORT, R.I., has this early paraphrase in
America of the epitaph of Edward the Black Prince, son
of Edward III of England, who died in 1376. (A varia-

tion, usually a couplet, was popular in New England and appears as late as 1873.):

> Josiah Lyndon
> Died Augt 8   1709
>
> Behovld and See
> For as I am Soe shalt Thov Bee
> Bvt as Thov Art
> Soe Once Was I
> Bee Svre Of This
> That Thov Mvst Dye.

◄§ 11. DR. ISAAC BARTHOLOMEW, 1710, age (39?), Cheshire, Conn.:

> He that was sweet to my Repose
> Now is become a stink under my Nose.
> This is said of me
> So it will be said of thee.

◄§ 12. BOSTON, MASS.:

> Recompense Wadsworth A.M. First
> Master of ye Grammar Free School
> at ye North End of Boston Aged
> about 24 y-rs; Dyed June ye 9th 1713.

◄§ 13. NEWBURY, MASS.:

> Here lys ye body of Mr
> Daniel Noyes Who died March
> ye 15th   1716   Aged 42 yrs
> 4 mos & 16 d-ys.
>
> As you were, so was I
> God did call and I did dy
> Now Children all whos name is Noyes
> Make Jesus Christ
> Your only choyes.

6

14. MARCY HALE, 1719, age 38, Glastonbury, Conn.:

> Here lies one wh
> os life thrads
> cut asunder she
> was stroke dead
> by a clap of thunder.

15. NEWPORT, R.I.:

> Here lieth entombed the body of
> Abigail, wife of Mr George Wanton,
> who died May 12th 1726 in the 28th
> year of her age, having left five pledges
> of her love.

If tears alas could speak a husband's woe
My verse would streight in plaintif numbers flow;
Or if so great a loss deplored in vain
Could solace so my throbbing heart from pain
Then would I, oh sad consolation, chuse
To soothe my cureless grief a private muse;
But since thy well known piety demands
A publick monument at thy George's hands
O Abigail I dedicate this tomb to the
Thou dearest half of poor forsaken me.

16. DEERFIELD, MASS.:

> Here lies the body of
> Lieut. Mehuman Hinsdell
> Died May 9 1736 in the 63d
> year of his age

He was the first male child born in this place &
was twice captivated by the Indian Salvages.
Blessed are the Merciful, for they
shall obtain Mercy.

~§ 17. JAMES PARK, 1741, age 36, Groton, Mass.:

He died no Libertine.
There is two extremes the world has always
run into since ye fall of Adam. 1st, Papists
here have exseded in boundlesse domination
& tyranny over ye consciences of men & what
ever is contrary to lawlesse decrees of ther
Councells & Popes is an unexpiatable heresie
& cannot be purged but by fire & fagot.
2. Whoever refuse subjection of conscience
to that Enemy of Christ, & to that woman-mistress
of witchcraft on whose skirts is found ye blood
of ye martyrs of Jesus, is presently an Heretick
& his arguments answered with burning quick.
This Tyranny over conscience we disclaim;
yet for that ought not ye other extremity
of wild toleration be embraced.

~§ 18. PALMER, MASS.:

Margaret daur. of Lt. William
and Abigail Scott Died Novr. 11,
1748 with ye mortal throat distemper
AE. 1 yr. 11 mos. 16 dys.

~§ 19. PLYMOUTH, MASS.:

This stone is erected to the Mem. of that
unbiased Judge, faithful officer sincere friend
and honest man, Col Isaac Lothrop, who resigned his
life on the 26th day of April 1750 in the 43d year
of his age.

Had Virtue's charms the power to save
His faithful Votaries from the grave
This stone would ne'er possess the fame
Of being marked with Lothrop's name.

ᘛ§ 20. CHESTER, N.H.:

Here Lies the body of
Mrs Jean Wilson
Spous of the Revd John Wilson
Who departed this Life April 1
AD 1752 Aged 36 years.
She was a Gentlewoman of Piety
& a Good Oeconamist
Likewise the Revd John Wilson
Who departed this Life Feby 1
AD 1779 Aged 69 years.

He was a Servant of Christ in the most
Peculiar & Sacred Relation, both in Doctrine &
Life. It was his great Delight to Prich a Crucefied
Christ as our Wisdom, Righteousness, Sanctification
& Redemption. He did not entertain his hearers
with Curiosities but Real Spiritual
Good. His Sermons were clear, solid,
Affictionate. A Spirit of vitall Christianity
ran through them. His Life was Sutable to
his holy Profession. He was a steady Friend a
loving Husband a Tender parent. His Inward
Grace was visable in a convercation
become the Gospel.
[One Night awaits us all; Death's road we
all must go. Horace]

9

✑§ 21. BOSTON, MASS. (Benjamin Franklin is the youngest son referred to on the original stone and the illustrious
author cited on its replacement in 1827):

Josiah Franklin
and
Abiah his wife,
Lie here interred,
They lived lovingly together in wedlock
Fifty-five years.
And without an estate or any gainful employment,
By constant labor and honest industry,
Maintained a large family comfortably,
And brought up thirteen children and seven
Grandchildren reputably.
From this instance, reader,
Be encouraged to diligence in thy calling,
And distrust not Providence.
He was a pious and prudent man;
She a discreet and virtuous woman.
Their youngest son,
In filial regard to their memory,
Places this stone.
J. F. Born 1655, Died 1744, AE. 89.
A. F. Born 1667, Died 1752, AE. 85.

The original inscription having been nearly
Obliterated
A number of citizens
Erected this monument, as a mark of respect
For the
Illustrious author,
MDCCCXXVII.

◄§ 22. FELCHVILLE, VT.:

On the 31st of
August 1754
Capt James
Johnson had
a Daughter born
on this spot of
Ground being
Captivated with
his whole Family
by the Indians

this is near the spot
that the Indians Encamped the
Night after they took Mr Johnson &
Family Mr Laberee & Farnsworth
August 30th 1754. And Mrs
Johnson was Delivered of her Child
Half a mile up this Brook.

When troubles near the Lord is kind,
He hears the Captives crys.
He can subdue the savage mind
And learn it sympathy.

*§ 23. BROOKLINE, MASS. (The technique referred to was direct infection from smallpox tissue or secretions, not that of vaccination with cowpox discovered by Dr. Edward Jenner in 1798):

> Sacred to the Memory of
> doctor Zabdiel Boylston, esqr.
> physician and Fellow of the Royal Society
> who first introduced the practise of
> inoculation into America.

> Through a life of extreme beneficence
> he was always faithful to his word, just
> in his dealings, affable in his manners;
> & after a long sickness in which he was
> exemplary for his patience and resignation
> to his Maker he quitted this Mortal Life
> in a just expectation of happy Immortality
> on the first day of March A.D. 1766
> Aetatis 87.

*§ 24. JOHN KENDALL, 1759, age 63, Dunstable, Mass.:

> Life is a Blessing can't be sold
> The Ransom is too high,
> Justice will ne'er be brib'd with gold
> That man may never die.
> You see the Foolish & the Wise
> The Tim'rous & the Brave
> Quit their Possessions, close their eyes
> And hasten to the Grave.

25. NEW HAVEN, CONN. (—but his religious narrow-mindedness so antagonized the students that they rioted, and the trustees forced him to resign):

> Here Lyeth Interred the Body of
> The Reverend and Learned
> Mr Thomas Clap
> The Late President of Yale College
> In New Haven
> A Truly Great Man

A Gentleman of A Superior Natural
Genius Most Asiduous Application
And Indefatigable Industry.
In the various Branches of Learning
He greatly Excell'd; An Accomplished
Instructor—A Patron Of the College
—A great Divine—bold for the Truth
—A zealous Promoter and Defender
of the Doctrines of Grace, of unaffected
Piety and a Patern of every Virtue.
The tenderest of Fathers and best of
Friends—the Glory of Learning and
an Ornament of Religion For 13
year the Faithfull and much Respected
Pastor of the Church in Windham:
And Near 27 years Laborious and
Painfull President of the College.
And having Served His own Genera-
tion by the Will of God With serenity
and calmness He fell on sleep the 7th day
of Janry 1767 In his 64th year
Death! Great Proprietor of All
'Tis thine to tread out Empires,
And to Quench the Stars.

⊷§ 26. CAPT. E. GRIFFIN, 1767, Madison, Conn. (—and same sentiments inscribed later for seamen in Boston and Newbury, Mass.):

> Tho Boreas' blasts and Boistrous waves
> Have tost me too and fro
> In spite of both, by God's decree
> I harbor here below.
> While I do now At Anchor ride
> With many of our Fleet
> Yet once again I must set Sail
> My Admiral Christ to meet.

⊷§ 27. LITCHFIELD, CONN.:

> Here lies the body of Mrs. Mary wife
> of Dea. John Buel Esq. She died
> Nov. 4   1768   AEtat. 90
> Having had 13 children
> 101 grand-children
> 274 great-grand-children
> 49 great-great-grand-children
> 410 Total. 336 survived her.

⊷§ 28. BOSTON, MASS.:

> Here lies ye body of
> Mrs. Ammey Hunt wife of
> Mr. Benjamin Hunt
> Who died Nov. 26th 1769
> Aged 40 years.

> A sister of Sarah Lucas lieth here,
> Whom I did love most Dear,
> And now her Soul hath took its Flight
> And bid her Spightful Foes good Night.

29. BENJAMIN BROOKS, 1769, age 22, Woburn, Mass.:

A loving husband to his wife
A Tender Parent two
Greatly lamented was his Death
By friend and kindred two.
The Lord was pleased to coll him home
Twas by the falling of a tree
And by a suding blow
To his long home did Go.
And now he slumbers in the dust
And will not rise before
The Lord the Judge desend from Heav'n
And Time shall be no more.

30. BOSTON, MASS.:

Here lies buried in a
Stone Grave 10 feet deep
Capt Daniel Malcom Mercht
who departed this Life
October 23d 1769
Aged 44 Years.

a true son of Liberty
a Friend to the Publick
an Enemy to oppression
and one of the foremost
in opposing the Revenue Acts
on America

⋖§ 31. SCOTLAND, CONN. (—mainly of interest because the gravestone was designed and cut by her grandson):

> Her Lyes ye Body
> of Mrs. Abigail Wife
> to Capt. John Man-
> ning Who Depart-
> ed this Life July
> 30th 1770 in ye 73d
> year of her Age.
>
> . . .
>
> *Made by Rockwell*
> *Manning aged 13 years*

⋖§ 32. BRATTLEBORO, VT. (—and similar wording occasionally elsewhere until 1802):

> Major John Arms, Esqr. Who Departed
> this life March ye 6th, 1770 in ye
> 48th year of his age.

> *Beneath the sacred Honours of the Tomb*
> *In awfull Silence and majestic Gloom*
> *The Man of Mercy here conceals his Head*
> *Amidst the awfull mansions of the Dead.*
> *No more his libral Hand shall help the Poor*
> *Relive Distress and scatter Joy no more.*

⋖§ 33. REPORTED FROM HEARSAY as in Hatfield, Mass., and Pownal, Vt., its model is obviously a longer version in Plymouth, England, 1750:

> Here lies as silent clay
> Miss Arabella Young
> Who on the 21st of May
> 1771
> Began to hold her tongue.

16

◄§ 34. HALIFAX, VT.:

> Mr. John Pannel killed by a tree
> In seventeen hundred & seventy three
>
> > When his father did come
> > He said Oh My Son
> > Your glass is run
> > Your work is done.

◄§ 35. CONCORD, MASS.:

> God wills us free—Man wills us slaves
> I will as God wills: Gods will be done.
> Here lies the body of
> John Jack
> A native of Africa who died
> March 1773, aged about sixty years.
>
> Tho born in the land of slavery
> He was born free:
> Tho he lived in a land of liberty
> He lived a slave
> Till by his honest tho stolen labours
> He acquired the source of slavery
> Which gave him his freedom:
> Tho not long before
> Death the great Tyrant
> Gave him his final emancipation
> And put him on a footing with kings.
> Tho a slave to vice
> He practised those virtues
> Without which kings are but slaves.

◆§ 36. DANIEL HOAR, 1773, age 93, Concord, Mass.:

> By Honest Industry &
> Prudent Oeconemy he acquired
> a handsome fortune for a man in
> Privet Carrecter. He enjoyed
> a long Life & uninterupted
> state of health, Blessings
> that ever attend [Scriptural]
> exersises & Temperance.

> Heres the last end of the Mortal Story
> He's Dead.

◆§ 37. NEW HAVEN, CONN.:

> Sacred
> to the Memory of
> Benjamin Douglas Esqr
> Barrister at Law & Kings Attorney
> For the County of Newhaven
> A Gentleman of the first Character
> For genuine Politeness, unbounded Hospitality
> Extensive Charity,
> and True Christian Benevolence;
> A Lawyer,
> Who with eminent Abilities in his Profession
> Preserved the most inviolate Reputation,
> For Integrity and Veracity
> And a Scorn of all the Chicanery
> of the Bar;
> A firm Friend to the Liberties of his Country,
> Whose true Interests he invariably pursued
> Without suffering himself to be drawn aside
> By the Allurements of Interest,

Or the Love of Popularity,
To countenance the destructive Measures
Of Ministerial Oppression on the one hand
Or Misguided Anarchy on the other.
He died December 3d. A. D. 1775
In the 36 Year of his Age.

Go Reader,
And in the short Space of Life allotted thee
Attend to his Examples
And Imitate his Virtues

38. BOSTON, MASS.:

Major John Pitcairn
Fatally wounded
while rallying the Royal Marines
at the Battle of Bunker Hill
was carried from the field to the boats
on the back of his son
who kissed him and returned to duty.
He died June 17 1775 and his body
was interred beneath this church.

19

*§ 39. The Westminster [Vt.] Massacre is the label Green Mountain history has accorded the deaths of William French and a seldom noted companion, and the event has often been cited as the first shots fired in the American Revolution, preceding the Battle of Lexington by nearly six weeks. At the time, though, the victims were perhaps more interested in resisting the "King's tools" as representing an attempt to extend New York State's jurisdiction to embrace their Connecticut River community, than they were concerned over the toryism of those who shot at them (*see also* Samuel Wells, No. 53).:

In Memory of William French
Son to Mr Nathaniel French
Who Was Shot at Westminster
March ye 13th 1775
by the hands of Cruel Ministereal Tools
of Georg ye 3d
in the Corthouse at a 11 a Clock at Night
in the 22d year of his Age.

Here William French his body lies
For Murder his blood for Vengance cries.
King Georg the third his Tory crew
tha with a bawl his head Shot Threw.
For Liberty and His Countrys Good
he Lost his Life his Dearest blood.

❧ 40. Noyan, Quebec:

Captain Remember Baker
Vermont Pioneer and Leader of the Green
Mountain Boys, was killed near this spot by Indians,
while on a scouting expedition in August 1775. He
was the first American killed in Canada, in the War
of the American Revolution.

His death made more noise in the country
then the loss of a thousand men towards
the end of the American War.   Ira Allen

❧ 41. Billerica, Mass.:

Here lies the body of widow Lydia Dyar of
Boston the place of her nativity, where she left
a good Estate & came into ye county May 22nd
1775 to escape ye abuce of ye Ministerial Troops,
sent by George ye 3rd to subject North America;
She died July 28th 1776, age 80 years.

The sweet remembrance of the just
Shall flourish when they sleep in Dust.

II. *1776 to 1815*

THE AMERICAN REVOLUTION is duly chronicled on Yankee gravestones. The War of 1812 is not: it was highly unpopular in New England, where merchant ship-owners and new textile manufacturers around Boston and Providence resented the embargoes, and settlers to the north and west smuggled briskly across the Canadian border until hostilities ceased in 1814.

Yet occasional markers reflect a far-from-storybook unanimity of spirit even during the rebellion. On the state level, Vermont declared herself an independent republic in 1777 with the avowed purpose of kicking off New York's jurisdiction, though she assured her "brethren in the United States of America" that she would, nevertheless, do her "full portion in maintaining and supporting the just war." She finally joined the Union as the fourteenth state in 1791.

War, Reason and Revivalism

Still another war—the French Revolution—had a profound effect on New England thought. Rationalism and the value of reason were ingredients of the 18th-century enlightenment which had encouraged the Colonies to fight for freedom. When France erupted in the name of liberty, equality and fraternity American free-thinkers applauded; their applause changed to disgust when the revolt merged into the Reign of Terror and finally into Napoleonic dictatorship. This, then, was what godless reason led to. The answer was a second Great Awakening.

However this time the revivalists were reacting against atheism and worldliness rather than against any particular doctrine of religion. The more emotional of their splinter sects were dismissed as "enthusiasts" by old-time moderates. The more solid among them would go on to lead the great humanitarian movements of the 19th century.

✒️ 42. LITTLE COMPTON, R.I. (twin stones):

In Memory of
Elizabeth who
should have been the
Wife of Mr
Simeon Palmer
who died Aug. 14th
1776 in the 64th Year
of her Age.

In Memory of
Lidia ye Wife of
Mr Simeon Palmer
who died Decem
ye 26 1754 in ye 35th
Year of her Age.

✒️ 43. RIDGEFIELD, CONN.:

In defense of American Independence
At the battle of Ridgefield, Apr. 27, 1777
Died Eight Patriots
Who were Laid in These Grounds
Companioned by
Sixteen British Soldiers;
Living, Their Enemies
Dying, Their Guests.

In Honor of Service and Sacrifice, this
Memorial is Placed For the
Strengthening of Hearts.

✒️ 44. ON ONE SIDE of a double stone commemorating
the deaths by lightning of two men, in Framingham,
Mass.:

In Memory of
Abraham Rice

Who departed this Life in a sudden
& Awful manner & we trust enterd
a Better June ye 3 Anno D. 1777 in
ye 81st Year of his Age.

My trembling Heart with Grief o'erflows
While I record the life of those
Who died by Thunder sent from Heaven
In Seventeen hundred & seventy seven.
Let all prepare for Judgement Day
As we may be Called out of Time
And in a sudden and awful way
While in our youth and in our Prime.

45. NEW HAVEN, CONN.:

Here
lies the Body of
Nathan Beers
who was born at Stratford & for the
last 25 Years of his Life was a respect-
able Inhabitant of this Town. He
received a mortal wound in his own
house from a party of the British
Troops in an Incursion they made to
this place July 5th 1779 with which he
languished till the 10th when he departed this Life in the 61th Year of his Age.

46. PLYMOUTH, MASS.:

To the memory of
Miss Hanna Howland
who died of a Languishment,
January ye 25th 1780   AEtatis 26.

For us they languish, & for us they die,
And shall they languish, shall they die in vain?

47. NORTH ATTLEBORO, MASS.:

Here lies the best of slaves
Now turning into dust
Caesar the Ethiopian craves
A place among the Just.
His faithful soul is fled
To realms of heavenly light,
And by the blood that Jesus shed
Is changed from Black to White.

Jany. 15 he quitted the stage
in the 77th year of his age.
1780

48. MIDDLETOWN, CONN.:

Joshua son of Mr Joshua & Mrs Anna
Miller who was killed with a
Sawmill May 26th AD 1781
In the 15th Year of his Age.

49. WETHERSFIELD, CONN.:

Here lie interred Mrs. Lydia
Beadle Aged 32 Years
Ansell Lothrop Elizabeth Lydia & Mary
Beadle her Children: the eldest aged
11 and the youngest 6 years Who
on the morning of the 11th day of Decr AD 1782
Fell by the hands of William Beadle
an infatuated Man who closed the
horrid sacrifice of his Wife
& Children with his own destruction.

Pale round their grassy tomb bedewd with tears
Flit the thin forms of sorrows and of fears:
Soft sighs responsive swell to plaintive chords
And indignations half unsheathe their swords.

₰ 50. FREDERICK JACKSON, 1778, age 1 year, Plymouth, Mass.:

> O happy Probationer! accepted without
> being exercised; it was thy peculiar
> privilege not to feel the slightest of
> those Evils, which oppress thy
> surviving kindred.

₰ 51. COLCHESTER, CONN.:

> Jonathan Kilborn
> Died Oct. 14, 1785   AEt. 79
>
> He was a man of invention great
> Above all that lived nigh
> But he could not invent to live
> When God called him to die.

₰ 52. MONTAGUE, MASS.:

> In Memory of Mr. Elijah Bardwell
> who died Janry 26th 1786 in ye 27th
> Year of his Age having but a few days
> surviv'd ye fatal Night when he was
> flung from his Horse & drawn by ye Stirrup
> 26 rods along ye path as appear'd by ye place
> where his hat was found & where he had
> Spent ye whole following severe cold night
> treading ye Snow in a small circle . . .

◄§ 53. BRATTLEBORO, VT. (This marble marker represents the last-ditch stand of a prominent resident who felt that York State should have jurisdiction over what was, at the time of his death, part of the independent and flourishing republic of Vermont.):

In Memory of Colo.
Samuel Wells of this town
a Judge of Cumberland
County Court & a Member
of the Assembly of the
Province of New York
who departed this Life
the 6th of August 1786 in
the 55th year of his Age.

have lost
His Friends the Stranger and the poor
Host.
A kind Companion and a gen'rous
When he fell the Statesman fell
And left the World his Worth to tell.

◄§ 54. NORWICHTOWN, CONN.:

> Alas, poor human nature!

> In Memory of Mr.
> Benjamin Butler
> who died of a Phthisis
> pulmonaris June 17th AD
> 1787 in the 48th year
> of his age.

◄§ 55. EZRA THAYER JACKSON, 1783, age 25 days, Plymouth, Mass.:

> What did the Little hasty sojourner
> find so forbidding & disgustful in
> our upper World to occasion its
> precipitant exit.

◄§ 56. MILFORD, CONN.:

> In Memory of Sarah Prudden
> who with a happier world in
> view departed this mortal state
> July 27 1788 in the 80th year of her age.

> Our age to seventy years is set
> How short the term how frail the state
> And if to eighty we arrive
> We rather sigh & groan than live.

◄§ 57. JABEZ GOODELL, a town father of Westminster, Vt., 1799, age 79, used the same verse with this difference:

> . . . And if to eighty we arrive
> We'd rather sigh and groan, and be alive.

⋙ 58. EIGHTY-ODD YEARS after his death, actually at the age of 52, a splendid monument was erected to the memory of the Hero of Ticonderoga and leader of the Green Mountain Boys—which doesn't mention the red-hot controversy he fostered with his skeptical treatise *Reason, the Only Oracle of Man.* This was the inscription on his first stone, which once stood near the present memorial in Burlington, Vt.:

The
Corporeal Part
of
Genl. Ethan Allen
rests beneath this stone
the 12th day of Feb. 1789,
aged 50 years.

His spirit tried the mercies of his God
In whom alone he believed and strongly trusted.

⋙ 59. WILLIAM KITTREDGE, 1789, age 91, Tewksbury, Mass.:

He's gone at length, how many grieve
Whom he did generously relieve
But o how shocking he expire
Amidst the flames of raging fire!
Yet all who sleep in Christ are bless'd
Whatever way they are undress'd.

⋙ 60. COVENTRY, CONN.:

This monument is erected in
Memory of Capt Joseph Talcott
who was Casually Drowned in the
Proud Waters of the Scungamug River
on the 10th Day of June 1789
in ye 62nd year of his age.

৶ 61. KENSINGTON, N.H.:

Serene and calm the mind in peace
His virtues shone with mild increase.

In Memory of
Benjamin Rowe Esq
Who after a Life of great usefullness
& patiently enduring 4 years ilness
with a dropsy underwent the Operation
of Tapping 67 times
From his body was drawn 2385 pounds of water
quietly departed this Life the 28 day
of March Anno Domini 1790 in
the 71st year of his age.

৶ 62. MARY HUMPHREY, 1791, age 36, Athol, Mass.:

My glass is run

With graceful & engaging mein
She trod the carpet & the green
With such refulgent virtues deckt
As gained her wide & warm respect.
Prim health sat blooming on her cheeks
Till Fortune play'd her cruel freaks
Her limbs in tort'ring pains confin'd
That wreck'd her joints tho not her Mind
By faith and patience fortified
The rudest tempest to abide
'Bove which she soar'd to realms of bliss
When Jesus hail'd her with a kiss.

᪥ 63. MARY FOWLER, 1792, age 24, Milford, Conn.:

Molly tho' pleasant in her day
Was suddenly seized and went away
How soon she's ripe, how soon she's rotten
Laid in her grave and soon forgotten.

᪥ 64. NEW HAVEN, CONN.:

In Memory of
Samuel Barns Son of
Mr Samuel Barns & Mrs
Welthy Barns whose
Death was Occasion'd
by a Scald from a Tea pot
March 27th 1794 aged 7
Months

Suffer little Children to Come unto
me and forbid them not for of
Such is the Kingdom of Heaven

❧ 65. HOLYOKE, MASS.:

> In Memory of
> Mr Nath. Parks,
> AEt 19, who on
> 21st March 1794
> Being out a hunt-
> ing and conceal'd
> in a Ditch was
> casually shot by
> Mr Luther
> Frink.

❧ 66. QUADRUPLETS in Danby Four Corners, Vt.:

> In Memory of four infants
> of Jacamiah & Mercy Palmer
> was born alive at one birth
> & died Nov. 25, 1795.

Four twen infants thay are dead
And laid in one silant grave
Christ took small infants in his arms
Such infants he will save.

❧ 67. BRATTLEBORO, VT.:

> this is in Memory of
> Mr Timothy Whipple,
> who departed this life
> November 4th, 1796
> in the 72nd Year
> of his Age.

Delirium's State was worse than fate,
And vacancy of mind;
But real grace fill'd up the space,
And left a hope behind.

⋖§ 68. Mrs. Sarah Newcomb, 1796, age 39, Keene, N.H.:

> How loved, how valued once avails thee not
> To whom related or by whom begot;
> A heap of dust alone remains of thee
> 'Tis all thou are, and what we all must be.

⋖§ 69. Dr. Polycarpus Cushman, 1797, age 47, Bernardston, Mass.:

> Vain censorius beings little know
> What they must soon experience below.
> Your lives are short, eternity is long;
> O think of death, prepare & then begone
> Thus art & Nature's powers and charms
> And drugs & receipts and forms
> Yield all, at last, to greedy worms,
> A despicable prey.

⋖§ 70. Mary Lefavour, 1797, age 74, Topsfield, Mass.:

> Reader pass on and ne'er waste your time,
> On bad biography and bitter rhyme
> For what I am this cumb'rous clay insures,
> And what I was, is no affair of yours.

There must be something magnetic about the place-name of Burlington: it seems to have attracted anthologers to a regular trove of questionable epitaphs, and each of the Burlingtons in Massachusetts, Vermont, Iowa and New Jersey is credited with one or more of the following inscriptions.

◄§ 71. Unbolstered by dates and reported as in Vermont or Iowa:

> Here lies our darling baby boy
> He never crys nor hollers.
> He lived for one and twenty days
> And cost us forty dollars.

◄§ 72. Also included as in Burlington, Mass. (—and reported, too, as in Burlington, N.J., but with the name as Mary Ann Lowder and without a date):

> Here lies the body of Susan Lowder
> Who burst while drinking a Sedlitz Powder.
> Called from this world to her heavenly rest,
> She should have waited till it effervesced.
>
> 1798

The main drawback to Miss Lowder's epitaph is that, according to *Remington's Practice of Pharmacy* (Easton, Pa., 1961), the preparation known as Seidlitz Powder was originated and patented in 1815, and remained a secret formula until published in 1824 by the Philadelphia College of Pharmacy.

◄§ 73. F. W. JACKSON, 1799, age 1, Plymouth, Mass.:

> Heav'n knows What man
> He might have made But we;
> He died a most rare boy.

◄§ 73. RANDOLPH CENTER, VT. (—a fairly modern stone to honor a country singing-master whose name is perpetuated in the first American breed of horse):

Justin Morgan
1747   1798
This man brought to
Vermont the colt from
which all Morgan Horses
are descended.

◄§ 74. SEVERAL VERSIONS are reported as in Lincoln, Me.:

Sacred to the Memory of Mr
Jared Bates who Died Aug. the 6th
1800. His Widow aged 24 who mourns
as one who can be comforted lives
at 7 Elm street this village
and possesses every qualification
for a good Wife.

◄§ 75. SURRY, N.H.:

In Memory of miss
Lucina willcox, who
Died May 7th 1800
aged 20 years.

Death is a debt
by nature due;
I've paid my shot,
And so must you.

⋘ 76. BRATTLEBORO, VT.:

In memory of John
Sergeant son of Mr Eli
& Betsey Sergeant
who Departed this
life Jan. 6th 1800 Aged
12 years 9 months
& 20 Days

These are words spoke by
His own mouth a few
Days Before his Death:—

The Spoiler is Among the
works of God. All that is
made must be Distroyed.
And all that is Born must
Die.

⋘ 77 & 78. JAFFREY, N.H.:

Sacred to the Memory of Amos Fortune
who was born free in Africa
a slave in America, he purchased
liberty, professed Christianity,
lived reputably, died hopefully
Nov. 17 1801 AEt. 91.

Sacred to the Memory of Violate
by purchase the slave of Amos Fortune
by marriage his wife, by her
fidelity his companion and solace
She died his Widow Sept. 13 1802 AEt. 73

❧ 79. CHIEF ORONO of the Penobscot Indians, 1801, age over 100, reportedly buried in Old Town, Me.:

> Safe lodged within his blanket here below
> Lies the last relics of Old Orono.
> Wore down with care, he in a trice
> Exchanged his Wigwam for a Paradise.

❧ 80 & 81. TWIN STONES in Grafton, Vt.:

In Memory of
Thomas K Park Junr
and thirteen infants.
Children of Mr.
Thomas K. Park and
Rebecca his wife

Youth behold and shed a tear.
Se fourteen children slumber
  here.
Se their image how they shine.
Like flowers of a fruitful vine.

In Memory of Mrs.
Rebecca Park wife of
Mr. Thomas K. Park.
who Died Septr 23d
1803 in the 40th year
of her age.

Behold and se as you pass by.
My fourteen children with me
  lie.
Old or young you soon must
  die
And turn to dust as well as I.

❧ 82. KITTERY POINT, ME.:

> Margaret Hills
> consort of
> Oliver Hills.
> died Oct. 31st 1803
> AEt. 28.

I lost my life in the raging Seas
A Sovreign God does as he please.
The Kittery friends they did appear
And my remains lie buried here.

❧ 83. KEENE, N.H.:

> In Memory of
> Mrs. Zilpah Kilburn wife
> of Mr. Jehiel Kilburn
> Who died Dec. 27 1804
> in the 22d year of her age.

> *Made by Moses*
> *Wright of Rockingham*
> *price six Dollars*

❧ 84. PLYMOUTH, MASS.:

Fanney Crombie daughter of Mr Calvin
Crombie & Mrs Naomi his wife
Departed this Life June 25th
A D 1804 in the 8th year
of her Age.

As young as beautiful! and soft as young.
As gay as soft; and innocent as gay!

A NUMBER of early residents of what is now Vernon, Vt., owe their continuing fame to epitaphs composed by the Rev. Bunker Gay, chronicler on stone for most of the Tutes, the Strattons and the Bridgemans.

◄§ 85. Gay's tribute to the real-life heroine, née Sartwell, of *Not Without Peril*, a novel of Indian captivity:

Mrs. Jemima Tute
Successively Relict of Messrs.
William Phipps Caleb Howe & Amos Tute
The two first were killed by the Indians
Phipps July 5th AD 1743
Howe June 27th 1755
When Howe was killed She & her Children
Then seven in number
Were carried into Captivity
The oldest a Daughter went to France
And was married to a french Gentleman
The youngest was torn from her Breast
And perished with Hunger
By the aid of some benevolent Gent'n
And her own personal Heroism
She recovered the Rest
She had two by her last Husband
Outlived both him & them
And died March 7th 1805 aged 82
Having past thro more vicissitudes
And endured more hardships
Than any of her Cotemporaries.
No more can Savage Foes annoy
Nor aught her widespread Fame Destroy.

◄§ 86. Jemima's first husband, William Phipps, has no marked grave, but the crudely lettered slate marker of her second husband is in Hinsdale, N.H.:

In Memory of Mr
Caleb How a very
Kind Companion who
Was Killed by the Indea
ns June the 27th
1755 in the 32d year
of his age his Wife Mrs
Jemima How With 7
Children taken Captive
at the Same time

Mr Caleb Howe Killed
was by Indeans 1755

❧ 87. Mr. Tute's elegant marble stone in Vernon,
Vt., beside Jemima's:

In Memory of
Mr. Amos Tute
who died April 17th
1790 in the 60th
Year of his
Age.

Were I so Tall to Reach the Pole
Or grasp the Ocean with my Span
I must be mesuer'd by my Soul
The Mind's the Standard of the
                                    Man.

◦§ 88. Behind his mother's, his epitaph like hers composed by the Rev. Mr. Gay, in Vernon, Vt.:

Here lies cut down like unripe fruit
A son of Mr. Amos Tute
And Mrs. Jemima Tute his wife
Called Jonathan of whose frail life
The days all summ'd (how short the account)
Scarcely to fourteen years amount
Born on the twelvth of May was he
In Seventeen Hundred Sixty Three
To death he fell a helpless prey
April the Five and Twentieth day
In Seventeen Hundred Seventy Seven
Quitting this world we hope for heaven
But tho his spirit's fled on High
His body mould'ring here must lie.
Behold the amazing alteration
Effected by inoculation
The means employed his life to save
Hurried him headlong to the grave!
Full in the bloom of youth he fell
Alas! what human tongue can tell
The Mother's Grief her Anguish show
Or paint the father's heavier woe
Who now no nat'ral offspring has
His ample fortune to possess
To fill his place, stand in his stead
Or bear his name when he is dead
So God ordained. His ways are just
Tho' Empires Crumble into dust
Life and this World mere Bubbles are
Set lose to this for Heaven prepare.

◦§ 89. Another by Gay, and in Vernon:

Here lies interred where Silence reigns
Mr. John Stratten's Sad Remains
Samuel and Ruth once happy were

In Him their only Son & Heir.
In January e'er the Sun
Had eight and twenty Circuits run
In Seventeen Hundred Fifty-six
With Mortals here on Earth to Mix
He first began, but lost his life
In Seventeen hundred eighty-five
The first of June as on his Tour
Where Walpole Rapids form a roar
He to a Rock went down too nigh
To peirce the Salmon passing by
The Rock's Smooth Glossy Sloping Side
His feet betray'd and let him slide
Plumb down into a watery tomb—
No more to see his Native Home
His tender Parents, lovely Spouse
Or those bright beauties of his House
Three little hapless female Heirs
Left to bedew his grave with Tears
Alas who can their loss repair
Or ease the widow's Soul of Care
Or furnish adequate Relief
To cure the Parent's pungent Grief
Father of mercies, hear our Call
Extend thy Pity to them all
Let Momentary Ills like this
Issue in everlasting bliss.

◄§ 90. And still another:

The unfortunate Miranda, dau. of John
& Ruth Bridgman, whose remains are here
interred, fell a prey to the flames that
consumed her father's house on ye 11th of June
1797, age 28.

> The rooms below flamed like a stove,
> Anxious for those that slept above,
> She ventured on ye trembling floor
> She fell; she sunk; and rose no more.

◄§ 91. Perhaps it says all he wanted said—or perhaps there was no one left to give him the full treatment he had accorded to his neighbors on either side of the Connecticut River; in Hinsdale, N.H.:

Mem. Mor.
Rev'd.
Bunker Gay
Obiit. Oct. 20
A.D. 1815 AEtatis 80

Be thou faithful unto death
And I will give thee a crown of gold.

I have fought a good fight
I have finished my course.

◄§ 92. JAMES RICHEY, 1806, age 51, Peterborough, N.H.:

A coffin, sheat & grave's
My earthly store
Tis all I want & kings
Can have no more.

◄§ 93. MARY ANN WRIGHT, 1808, age 1 year, Hinsdale, N.H.:

Come little children see the place
Where infant dust must lie
There is no age thats free from this
Both young and old must die.

94. THE REV. NATHAN NOYES, 1808, Windham, Vt.:

Look here and view affliction's favorite son
For Misfortune through all my life has run
Hard perfection's iron yoke I bore
Till I have seen of gloomy years, three score.
Now shout in vain, ye persecuting throng
I'm far beyond the poison of your song
Live and live happy while my grave you view
This tongue, now cold, has often prayed for you.

95. CAPT. THOMAS PRENTICE, 1809, age 72, Newton Centre, Mass.:

He that's here interr'd needs no versifying,
A virtuos life will keep his name from dying;
He'll live tho poets cease their scribling rhym
When that this stone shall moulderd be by time.

96. ANNA EVEANS, 1809, age 24, Hinsdale, N.H.:

Nine vastly painful years she passed
Calm and serene from first to last,
Hard was her struggle, long the strife
Between her malidy and life.
Af length as both together ended
Her patient soul to Heaven ascended;
Exchanged a Life of great distress
To one of Endless happiness.

97. VERNON, VT.:

Dill Elmer
died Jan. 11 1804 AEt. 67

Tranquil & silent here lies Dill,
What gifts he had he managed well.
He did his best to merit fame
And left behind him a good name.
Remember Dill and do the same.

⋙ 98. NEWBURY, MASS.:

Here lies
In a state of perfect oblivion
John Adams
who died Sept 2 1811
AE 79

Death has decomposed him
And at the great resurrection Christ
will recompose him.

⋙ 99. CAROLINE NEWCOMB, 1812, age 4 months, Martha's Vineyard, Mass. (—and also found in New Hampshire and Vermont.):

She tasted Life's bitter cup
Refused to drink the portion up
But turned her little head aside
Disgusted with the taste and died.

⋙ 100. WEST BRATTLEBORO, VT.:

Rhoda Nash
(a pattern of Amiableness)
Who died Nov. 26, 1813 AE. 23 years

If my Earthly hope has been cut off in forming
an endearing connection in this World, yet a
Heavenly hope revives, that I shall form a more
glorious connection in a better world.

⋙ 101. INFANT SON of Timothy Hoskins Jr, 1813, Westmoreland, N.H. (—also found in Vermont):

This rose was sweet awhile
Now it is odour vile.

❧ 102. GRAFTON, VT. (—and although many stone-cutters signed their handiwork it's unusual to see an advertisement for a shaky chisel):

In Memory of Mr Ebenezer Tinney
who died March 12, 1813, aged 81 yrs.

My virtue liv's beyond the grave
My glass is rum.

Made by A. Wright & A. Burditt
B. Falls AD 1813

❧ 103. CLAREMONT, N.H.:

In Memory of
Chester and Elisha Putnam sons of
the late Capt. Solomon Putnam, who
on the morning of January 29th 1814
in the same bed were found suffocated.
A kettle of common coals having been
placed in their room for comfort
proved the fatal instrument of their
deaths; the former in the 27th the
latter in the 19th year of his age.

How many roses perish in their bloom,
How many suns alas go down at noon.

❧ 104. JONAS TEMPLE, 1815, age 80, Boylston, Mass.:

His private character was pure;
allowing for human frailties
his Christian life was unblemished.

◂§ 105. FOR A SHOE-MENDER, 1815, Weathersfield, Vt.:

Beneath here lies a mender of the Sole
Whose like you will not find from pole to pole.
By every honest means he got his Awl
And happy could he live tho' in a Stall;
His Ends he answer'd in this life that's past
And now let's hope he's happy at the Last.

◂§ 106. YORK, ME. (A civil engineer, Major Sewall is credited with designing America's first pile bridge, a 270-foot structure across the York River with a central draw-span through which coastal shipping could sail upriver. The bridge at York—which also was the first such crossing in the New World to be built on a plan resulting from a survey of its site beforehand—inspired similar bridges in the Colonies and Ireland.):

In memory of
Major Samuel Sewall;
An architect of the first class,
From whose fabrications great benefits
have resulted to society;
He was benevolent, hospitable, and
generous, without ostentation,
and pious without enthusiasm.

He died July 23d, 1815. AEt. 91.

III

1816 to 1870

The Age of Ferment

ABOLITION of slavery was the greatest single cause embraced by New Englanders during the fifty-odd years from 1816 through the Civil War. Though the earliest slavers had sailed from Massachusetts and Rhode Island —and Southerners never ceased to mention the fact— Vermont's constitution in 1777 was the first to outlaw slaveholding, and the proportionately few slaves owned by Yankees were domestic servants rather than a labor supply necessary to the region's economy. Thus when social reformers and evangelist groups began their drive against slavery in the 1820's they could do so in the name of humanity. By 1860 the issue had become a matter of saving the nation, and Yankee response was so strong that New Hampshire led the entire North in the number of Union soldiers per thousand of population who were killed in battle during the Civil War.

Meanwhile New England's intellectual/emotional climate had fostered other movements, some lasting and some outlandish. The most virulent was antimasonry, which prompted Vermont to give her electoral votes for the Presidency to the anti-Mason candidate in 1832 and to reelect for three terms a governor who ran as a foe of Freemasons. The cause lost momentum after 1840 and Gov. William A. Palmer's epitaph, inscribed in 1860, details his career but ignores his political bias.

Temperance, prison reform, public education and self-improvement: all flourished in an age that believed man was innately good and that the sky was the limit to his nobility if proper scope was offered in place of temptation. Missionary societies abounded. New religions sprang forth almost full grown—the Mormons, the Adventists, the Perfectionists, faith-healers and Spiritists.

The Industrial Revolution played its part too, and epitaphs commemorate such Yankee innovations as steam power in factories and bigger bridges and the Colt revolver. In general, however, the rise of the mass-communication industry seems to have throttled the old desire to say one's say on a tombstone. Maybe it was the spread of finer feelings and maybe it was just a new self-consciousness. Whatever the reason, at the end of this period the early outspokenness that tells so much was on its way out and nice-Nellyism, unrevealing and bland, was on its way in.

⊷§ 107. ELISHA WOODRUFF, 1816, age 70, Pittsford, Vt.:

> How shocking to the human mind
> The log did him to powder grind.
> God did command his soul away
> His summings we must all obey.

⊷§ 108. DR. GEORGE FARRINGTON, 1816, age 47, Chester-field, N.H.:

> Here lies beneath this monument
> The dear remains of one who spent
> His days and years in doing good,
> Gave ease to those opress'd with pain,
> Restor'd the sick to Health again
> And purified their wasting blood.
> He was respected while on Earth
> By all who knew his real worth,
> In practice and superior skill.
> The means he used were truly blest,
> His wondrous cures will well attest.
> Who can his vacant mansion fill,
> Bourne on some shining cherub's wing
> To his Grand Master, God & King
> To the Grand Lodge in Heaven above
> Where angels smile to see him join
> His brethren in that Lodge Divine
> Where all is Harmony & Love.

⊷§ 109. NEWPORT, R.I.:

> In Memory of Samuel Moses
> Who died Sept. 17, 1817 aged 47 yrs.

Man comes into the world naked and bare
He travels through life with trouble & care
His exit from the world no one knows where
If it's well with him here, it is well with him there.

110. HARVARD, MASS.:

In memory of
Capt. Thomas Stetson
Who was killed by the fall of
a tree Nov. 28 1820 AE. 68

Nearly 30 years he was master
of a vessel and left that
employment at the age of
48 for the less hazardous
one of cultivating his farm.
Man is never secure from
the arrest of death.

111. BURLINGTON, VT.:

James Savage, who died
in his seat in Plattsburgh, N. Y.
June 8, 1821
in the 85th year of his life.

This modest stone, what few vain marbles can,
With truth may say, Here lies an honest man.
Calmly he looked on either life, and here
Saw nothing to regret; nothing there to fear.

112. SIDNEY SNYDER, 1823, age 20, Providence, R.I.:

The wedding day
decided was,
The wedding wine
provided;
But ere the day did
come along
He'd drunk it up and
died, did.
Ah Sidney! Ah Sidney!

⋙ 113. ACWORTH, N.H.:

> This stone tells the death of
> Bezaleel Beckwith
> not where his body lies.
> He died Oct. 31, 1824, aged 43.
> The thirteenth day after, his body
> was stolen from the grave.
>
> Now twice bereaved the mourner cries,
> My friend is dead, his body gone;
> God's act is just, my heart replies,
> Forgive, oh God, what man has done.
>
> Erected by the friends of the deceased in
> Acworth in place of one destroyed by some
> ruthless hand in April, 1825.

⋙ 114. WINSLOW, ME.:

> Here lies the body of Richard Thomas
> an inglishman by birth
> A Whig of '76
> By occupation a cooper
> now food for worms.
>
> Like an old rum puncheon whose
> staves are all marked, numbered and shooked
> he will be raised again and finished
> by his creator.
>
> He died Sept. 28, 1824. Aged 75.
>
> America my adopted country
> my best advice to you is this
> Take care of your liberties.

❦ 115. PLAINFIELD, VT.:

> Abial Ledoyt, son of
> Jacob and Polly Perkins
> who was drownded August 17, 1826
> aged 13 years & 14 days.

> This blooming Youth in Health most fair
> To his Uncle's Mill-pond did repaire,
> Undressed Himself and so plunged in
> But never did come out again.

❦ 116. JOSEPH HILL (who must have admired Hayley's poem about a blacksmith), 1826, age 65, Norton, Mass.:

> My sledge and hammer be reclined
> My bellows too have lost their wind;
> My fire's extinguished, forge decay'd
> And in the dust my vice is laid.
> My iron's spent, my coals are gone,
> The last nail's drove, my work is done.

Gone Home

MEDICAL CARE is often mentioned on gravestones of the 1800's—not as a sideswipe at doctors, but to show that families saved no effort or expense to save a loved one.

⁂§ 117. Found in virtually every sizable graveyard in New England during the 19th century:

Affliction sore long time I bore
Physicians skill was vain.
Then God did send Death as a friend
To ease me from my pain.

⁂§ 118. Equally popular, with variations (except that it's always two doctors):

My sickness was severe
Twas long and tedious too
My childrens love was all in vain
Likewise physicians two.

⁂§ 119. These inscriptions, coupled with ones like that of Leverett Kimball, 1826, age 18 months, Keene, N.H., could be the inspiration for the flip "forty-dollar-baby" (No. 71) that's more folklore than fact:

With anxious care each art was tried
The lovely flower to save.
But all in vain—the shaft of death
Consigned it to the grave.

⁂§ 120. EBENEZER SCOTT, 1826, age 83, Vernon, Vt.:

Grandfather

The first white male born in Bernardston,
Mass. Was taken with his mother and two brothers
by the Indians, carried to Quebec, sold to the
French when he was 8 years old. Returned to his
father. Served in the Revolution—drew a pension.

๙ 121. PLYMOUTH, MASS.:

Bathsheba James, wife of Capt.
William Holmes 3d Mariner and daughter
to Capt. Joseph Doten, Ditto. She was
kill'd instantaneously in a Thunder storm
by the Electrich fluid of lightning on
the 6th day of July 1830, aged 36 yrs & 26 dys.

She was an affectionate Wife, a dutiful
Daughter, a happy mother, a kind and sincere
Friend. Alas sweet Blossom short was the
period that thy enlivening virtues contributed
to the Happiness of those connections,
But O how long have they to mourn the loss of
so much worth and Excellence.

๙ 122. MRS. MARTHA HERRICK, age 44, and her 9-month-
old daughter, both in 1830, Blue Hill, Me.:

Insatiable death will have his pray
Nor youth, nor age his mighty grip can stay:
The Mother falls beneath his power
And soon her infant's forced to cower.

◄§ 123. PLYMOUTH, MASS.:

> In memory of Nancy Williams
> A faithful (African) servant in the
> family of Rev. F. Freeman, died
> Nov. 31, 1831, aged 25 years.

Honour and shame from no conditions rise:
Act well your part—there all honour lies.

◄§ 124. PLYMOUTH, MASS.:

> Sacred to the memory of
> Miss Sally C. Robbins, dau'r of
> Capt. Samuel & Mrs. Sarah Robbins
> She decea'd by a fall from a
> chaise Aug. 14, 1828, aged 25 years
> 5 mo's and 10 days.

Our home is in the grave:
Here dwells the multitude; we gaze around,
We read their monument, we sigh; and while
we sigh, we sink.

◄§ 125. JOHN KERR, 1835, age 46, Providence, R.I.:

I dreamt that buried in my fellow clay
Close by a common beggar's side I lay;
Such a mean companion hurt my pride
And like a corpse of consequence I cried:
Scoundrel begone, and henceforth touch me not,
More manners learn, and at a distance rot.
Scoundrel, in still haughtier tones cried he,
Proud lump of earth, I scorn thy words and thee:
All here are equal, thy place now is mine;
This is my rotting place, and that is thine.

126. MARY S. HOYT, 1836, Bradford, Vt.:

She lived—what more can then be said:
She died—and all we know she's dead.

127. WINSLOW, ME.:

In Memory of
Beza. Wood
Departed this life
Nov. 2, 1837
Aged 45 yrs.

Here lies one Wood
Enclosed in wood
One Wood
Within another.
The outer wood
Is very good:
We cannot praise
The other.

128. WILLIAM DEERING, 1839, age 49, Orient, Me.

For me the world hath had its charms
And I've embraced them in my arms,
Courted its joys and sought its bliss
·Although I knew the end was this.

129. JONATHAN TILTON, 1837, age 66, Chilmark, Mass.:

Here lies the body of Jonathan Tilton
Whose friends reduced him to a skeleton.
They robbed him out of all he had
And now rejoice that he is dead.

◄§ 130. ALBERT FULLER, 1838, age 16, Putney, Vt.:

> *His death was occasioned by*
> *an accidental blast of powder*
> *on July 4th.*

◄§ 131. CAPT. THOMAS COFFIN, 1842, age 50, New Shoreham, R.I.:

> *He's done a-catching cod*
> *And gone to meet his God.*

◄§ 132. BRATTLEBORO, VT.:

> *Experiance*
> *relict of Samuel*
> *Wellington, died*
> *Dec. 17, 1838.*
> *AE. 69.*
> *her first husband*
> *was Elias Bemis.*

◄§ 133. NEW IPSWICH, N.H.:

> *Mr Gilman Spaulding*
> *Was kill'd with an axe*
> *By an insane Brother*
> *Sept. 19, 1842.*
> *Aet. 38.*

◄§ 134. PATIENCE HOLMES, 1845, age 24, Plymouth, Mass. (—and others in New Hampshire and Vermont):

> Shed not for her the bitter tear
> Nor give the heart to vain regret
> 'Tis but the casket that lies here
> The gem that filled it sparkles yet.

◄§ 135. PUTNEY, VT.:

> Charles Henry Gilson
> son of
> Xenophon & Mary
> Gilson, Died
> April 18, 1845
> AE 6 yrs 3 mo 20 ds
> He was instantly killed
> by a stagecoach passing
> over him.

> This lovely flower of fairest bloom
> Thus early met a sudden doom
> From his fond parents torn away
> Now lives and blooms in endles' day.

◄§ 136. HERMON FIFE, 1845, age 45, North Pembroke, N.H.:

> Here lies the man
> Never beat by a plan
> Straight was his aim
> And sure of his game
> Never was a lover
> But invented the revolver.

🖙 137. YANKEES played a major part in the spread of whaling in the Atlantic and Pacific—until petroleum was discovered in the United States in 1859 and kerosene thereafter took over as the leading fuel for lamps—and their epitaphs can be read in profusion around Nantucket and New Bedford, with even one so far inland as Hinsdale, N.H. In Montville, Conn.:

> *Daniel Chappell*
> *Who was killed in the act*
> *of taking a whale*
> *October 15, 1845*
> *age 25 years.*
> *Blessed are they that die in the Lord.*

🖙 138. POWNAL, VT.:

> *Solomon Towslee Jr*
> *Who was kill'd in Pownal*
> *Vt. July 15, 1846, while*
> *repairing to Grind a sithe*
> *on a stone atach'd to the*
> *Gearing in the Woollen*
> *Factory. he was entangled.*
> *his death was sudden & awful.*

🖙 139. JOSEPH SHELDEN, 1847, age 42, Canton, Mass.:

> *I was a stout young man*
> *As you might see in ten;*
> *And when I thought this*
> *I took in hand my pen*
> *I wrote it down plain*
> *That everyone might see*
> *That I was cut down like*
> *A blossom from a tree.*
> *The Lord rest my soul.*
> *Amen*

◄§ 140. SETH J. MILLER, 1848, age 46, Rehoboth, Mass.:

My wife from me departed
And robbed me like a knave
Which caused me broken hearted
To descend into my grave.
My children took an active part
And to doom me did contrive,
Which struck a dagger to my heart
Which I could not survive.

◄§ 141. THE REV. BEZALEEL PINNEO, 1849, age 80, Milford, Conn.:

During his ministry
He enjoyed 7 revivals,
Admitted 716 members,
Baptized 1,117 and
Buried 1,126 of his flock.

◄§ 142. RYEGATE, VT.:

In Memory of Alden Work.
He died July 1st in the 80th
year of the American era. He was
an active, honest, and successful
merchant, and a firm Democratic
representative in the Legislature
of Vermont. He died as he lived—happy.

I lived on Earth
I died on Earth
In Earth I am interred
All that have Life
Are sure of Death
The rest may be inferred.

✍ 143. Dr. JOHN W. RICHMOND, 1857, age 81, Stonington, Conn. (—where he moved in 1850):

When Rhode Island, By her Legislation
From 1843 to 1850
Repudiated her Revolutionary Debt
Dr. Richmond,
Removed from that state to this borough, and
selected this as his family Burial-place,
Unwilling that the remains of him-
self and family should be dis-
graced by forming part of a
Repudiating State.

✍ 144. THE VICTIM of an accident during construction of the 500-foot-long covered bridge of the Sullivan County Railroad, an engineering masterpiece in its day; Cuttingsville, Vt.:

William Pelsue
Died Aug. 2, 1851, aged 42 yrs.

He was killed at Bellows Falls, Vt.,
While raising a bridge across
The Connecticut River.

✍ 145. THE NATURE of the marker—a wooden slab on which were mounted a daguerreotype and an inscription on paper covered with glass—would indicate that it is no longer readable, even if it is still standing. However, John R. Kippax, in his anthology published in 1877, recorded the epitaph as in Southampton, Mass.:

This
inclosure was
dedicated to the ashes of
Josiah Gridley
and family
March 16, 1852.

The above likeness was taken of the family as it existed
Nov. 17th, 1847, with the exception of Mrs. G. who was
so deranged that it was impossible to take her with the
group. Albert J., the oldest son, laid off the Outer
Form Nov. 10, 1851, aged 19 years—yet he is neither dead
nor asleep, but converses daily with his friends in the
body, of the things that pertain to the kingdom of God.

◄§ 146. BETWEEN 1838 and 1847 Putney, Vt., was the
cradle of John Humphrey Noyes Jr's religious sect called
Perfectionism, whose more ardent members practiced
"animal magnetism" and "complex marriage." Less enlightened townsfolk reviled the Perfectionists as practicing
free love, and forced Noyes to leave for Oneida, N.Y.,
where he established the organization later renowned as
makers of Community Plate silverware. Mrs. Whiting's
stone in Putney, erected several years after the original
group had disbanded, is the only local marker to claim
membership explicitly in the society.:

Evalina E.
wife of
James L. Whiting
and a member of
The
Putney Community
Died Feb. 14, 18[53]
AE. 32 yrs.

I am persuaded that
neither death nor life
shall be able to sep-
arate us from the love
of God, which is in
Christ Jesus our Lord.

⋖ 147. Hanover, N.H.:

> Here lies the mortal wreck of
> Sally Dugby   AE 69 yrs.
>
> In the midst of society
> she lived alone.
> Beneath the mockery of cheer-
> fulness, she hid deep woe.
> In the ruin of her intellect
> the kindness of her heart
> survived.
>
> She perished in the snow on
> the night of Feb. 25, 1854.

⋖ 148. New Boston, N.H.:

> Sevilla,
> daughter of
> George & Sarah
> Jones
> Murdered by
> Henry N. Sargent
> Jan. 13, 1854.
> AEt. 17 yrs. & 9 mos.

Thus fell this lovely blooming daughter
By the revengeful hand—a malicious Henry
When on her way to school he met her
And with a six self cocked pistol shot her.

◄§ 149. Near by in the same New Boston cemetery, a suicide:

Henry N.
Son of Daniel and
Charlotte Sargent
Died Jan. 13, 1854
AEt. 23 yrs. & 5 mos.

Murderer of
Sevilla Jones

◄§ 150. BENJAMIN M. BURNHAM, 1855, age 58, Portsmouth, N.H.:

Originator of the Trite Swearing
Dead but yet speakest
Swear not at all.

To change to praise the swearer's wicked prayer
To show the love of God seemed all his care.
To keep away from human eye
The lights we see God's glory by.

◄§ 151. DUMMERSTON, VT.:

Gone Home
Adin N. French Died July 19
1855, AE. 29 years and 9 months.

The deceased came to his death by the
explosion of the Engine "John Smith" on the
Vermont and Canada Railroad, in Milton, Vermont.

A Husband kind a Father dear
A Friend in need lies buried here.

~§ 152. STEPHEN F. FASSETT, 1856, age 54, Winchendon, Mass.:

> I began the preserving
> of cow's milk with white
> sugar for the use of steamers
> crossing the Atlantic Ocean.

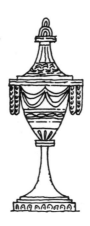

~§ 153. JAMES ANTHONY, Newport, R.I.:

> For Eighteen Years
> attached to the United States Navy.
> Died Dec. 9, 1857, in the 73rd year of his age.

> He spent his life upon the sea
> Fighting for the nation
> He doubled his enjoyment
> By doubling all his ration.

154. Dr. Alvin Lusk, 1858, age 75, West Berkshire, Vt.:

Name & Sentiments

A ll nature, self-existent powers innate
L ife gives & takes, forms, solves as adaptate,
V irtue obeys, Vice disobeys her laws,
I n that all good, this only evil draws
N o good or ill by supernatural cause.
L et not imagination take its flight
U pward to fancied regions for delight;
S cience & virtue lead to happiness—
K nown truth, not fantom faith, to bliss.

I have no fears because I've got
No faith nor hope in Juggenaut
Nor Yok, Grand Lama, Boud nor Zend,
Nor Bible systems without end,
Nor Alcoran nor Mormon views
Nor any creed that priest dupes use;
Each class self-pure condemns the rest,
Enlightened minds the whole detest;
In strongest faith no virtue lies,
An unbelief no vice implies.
A bare opinion hurts no man;
Then prove it hurts a God, who can
To others do, to others give
As you'd have done or would receive.

155. CRANSTON, R.I. (—to the man who introduced steam power into textile manufacturing, America's first major industry):

David Whitman
Died August 30, 1858
Aged 59 years.

A man
of mild and genial manners,
of wondrous skill in his profession,
combined with
kind and generous affections
and unspotted integrity.

This monument is erected
to his memory,
by his friends
and the friends of
American Industry.

156. PELHAM, MASS.:

Warren Gibbs
Died by arsenic poisoning
Mar. 23, 1860
Aged 36 yrs. 5 ms. 23 dys.

Think my friends when this you see
How my wife has done for me
She in some oysters did prepare
Some poison for my lot and fare
Then of the same I did partake
And Nature yielded to its fate.
Before she my wife became
Mary Felton was her name.

Erected by his brother
Wm. Gibbs

◆§ 157. GROTON, VT.:

Scott

In Memory of William Scott, The Sleeping Sentinel
Pardoned by Abraham Lincoln, Sept. 9, 1861.
Born on this farm Apr. 9, 1839
Enlisted in Company K, 3rd Vt. Volunteers
July 10, 1861
Died of Wounds at Lee's Mills, Va.
April 16, 1862.

◆§ 158. LURANA NICHOLS, 1863, age 51, Fletcher, Vt.
(—whose husband, Hilkiah P. Nichols, was in the Union
Army from 1862 to 1865):

Here lies the remains of H. P. Nichol's wife
Who mourned away her natural life.
She mourned herself to death for her man
While he was in the service of Uncle Sam.

◆§ 159. STANSTEAD, QUEBEC: (—one of the rare anti-
Lincoln inscriptions to derive from the pro-Union strong-
hold of northern New England; see also Joseph Brain-
nerd):

Eleazer Albee
Born in Rockingham, Vt.
Died in Stanstead Aug. 28, 1864

He went into Voluntary Banishment from his
Beloved Native Country, during the Reigning
Terror in the Third Year of the
Misrule of Abraham the First.

✥ 160. St. Albans, Vt.:

Joseph P. Brainerd
A Brave Soldier.

Joseph Partridge
Brainerd, son of
Joseph H. Brainerd
and his wife Fanny Part
ridge, a conscientious,
faithful, brave Union
Soldier, was born on the
27th day of June 1840,
graduated from the
University of Vermont
in August 1862, enlisted
into Co. L. of the Vermont
Cavalry, was wounded
and taken prisoner by the
Rebels in the Wilderness,
May 5, 1864, was sent to
Andersonville Prison
Pen in Georgia where he died
on the 11th day of Sept. 1864
entirely and wholly neglected by
President Lincoln and murdered
with impunity by the Rebels,
with thousands of our loyal
Soldiers by Starvation, Privation,
Exposure and Abuse.

MOST STONES of Union soldiers killed in the war bear verses or admonitions, as well as the units in which they served.

◄§ 161. Typical is the inscription for Corporal D. Learned, 1864, age 23, Dublin, N.H.:

Soldier rest, thy work is done:
Sharp the contest, fierce the strife,
The battle's fought, the victory won;
Thy sure reward, Eternal Life.

◄§ 162. William P. Eames, 1863, age 24, West Halifax, Vt.:

We mourn and lament our brave youth
In one deep and national wail,
Who rushed to support our dear old flag
In its hour of deepest travail.

◄§ 163. Lucius P. Miles, 1863, age 20, Williamsville, Vt.:

How sleeps the brave who sink to rest?
By all their country's wishes blest.

Whether on the tented field
Or in the battle's van,
The fittest place for man to die
Is where he dies for Man.

◄§ 164. On many New England markers:

A devoted martyr to the
Cause of his Country.
Reader, Art thou possessed of Liberty?
He died for thee.

✑§ 165. DUMMERSTON, VT. (see Proverbs 31:10-31):

Joanna Wilder
Born Mar. 10, 1785
Died Dec. 15, 1865
Aged 80 years, 8 months & 5 days.

She fulfilled in a good degree the
Scripture requirements for the wife
of a Deacon.
She lived with her husband 60 years.

✑§ 166. DUXBURY, MASS.:

Asenath

Widow of
Simeon Soule
Died
Feb. 25, 1865.
Aged
87 years, 11 mo.
& 19 days.

The Chisel can't help
her any.

◄§ 167. EDWARD OAKES, 1866, age 24, Middlebury, Vt.:

Faithful husband thou art
At rest untill we meet again.

◄§ 168. DOVER, N.H.:

Repository
of
Husband & Wife.

Joseph Hartwell, Inanimated
Apr. 7, 1867, AEt. 68.
Betsy Hartwell, Inanimated
Dec. 7, 1862, AEt. 68.

The following embraces a period of 41 years. In all of
our relations in life toward each other, there has been
naught but one continuation of fidelity and loving kind-
ness. We have never participated or countenanced in
others secretly or otherwise that which calculates to sub-
jugate the masses of the people to the dictation of the
few. And now we will return to our Common Mother with
our Individualities in life unimpaired, to pass through
together this ordeal of the earth's chemical Laboratory
preparatory to recuperation.

Her last exclamations.

If you should be taken away I could not survive you.
How happy we have lived together. O, how you will miss
me. Think not, Mr. Hartwell, I like you the less for being
in the situation you are now in. No, it only strengthens
my affections.

To those who have made professions of friendship and
have then falsified them by living act—Pass On.

❧ 169. EAST HAMPSTEAD, N.H.:

Thomas Gilbert,
died
Jan. 21, 1868.
AEt. 85 yrs.

The voice of a step Father.

Beneath this stone is to rest one
Shamefully robbed in life
By his wife's son, and Esquire Tom,
And Daniel Seavy's wife.

IV

1871 to the PRESENT

The Big New World

ONLY A LITTLE of the transition from gaslight to space capsules is noted in New England epitaphs, thanks to a fashion in gravestones that can best be described as the age of monuments.

Three things combined to start the trend: growing restraint in texts, decreasing room in cemeteries and the Victorian idea that opulence testified to grief and respect. Therefore in general the 1870's and 80's were peak years for big central stones, over-machined and elaborately lettered, rising high over the related tablets around them. Twentieth-century reaction against ornateness has produced simpler memorials of greater refinement; but lack of room, especially in cities, has encouraged the use of family markers carved with only a surname and the dates of members who are buried near by.

Another factor in the decline of individual stones bearing epitaphs is that communities have, after modern wars, erected public monuments honoring those in military service.

Still another reason for the recent moderation in Yankee inscriptions could be the simple one of cost. Records show that a skilled artisan received ten Spanish-milled dollars in 1790 for a pair of tombstones complete with longish epitaphs; whereas today's average charge for cutting each letter, aside from the price of the stone itself, is 65 cents if it's sand-blasted in the workshop and $1.25 if it's chiseled by hand in the graveyard.

Yet despite changing styles the old wish to report a fact or state a belief lingered on during these ninety years. The benefits of heaven, compared with the sorrows of mortal life, was the most popular text. Many a stone promises "We Shall Meet Again" or "Gone to Rest." Sometimes the message is more involved and may tell of "A gem, a precious jewel/ Placed in our Saviour's crown/ Twill blossom there in fragrance/ Safe from the world's cold frown"; or says that "The curse of flesh is here laid by/ Our Spirit is like the butterfly/ Free to drink of endless pleasure/ Upward, onward to our Saviour." Such inscriptions have dignity and value because they are where they are.

Also worth recording were the Grange movement, young and important in the 1870's; continuing interests in Spiritism, atheism, evangelism and temperance, new inventions and the discovery that the earth is flat.

♨ 170. MOTHER of the Eddys, who transmitted her powers as a medium to her famous Spiritist family, Chittenden, Vt. (—and near her house stood a marker in memory of her favorite contact in the other world, an Indian named Santum):

Our Mother
Julia A. Eddy
Wife of
Zephania Eddy

Entered the World
of Spirits
Dec. 29th, 1872
AE 59 y's, 9 m's, 24 d's.

♨ 171. JONATHAN RICHARDSON, 1872, age 82, East Thompson, Conn.:

Who never sacrificed his reason
at the altar of superstition's God,
who never believed that Jonah
swallowed the whale.

♨ 172. LEOMINSTER, MASS.:

Joseph Palmer
Died Oct. 30, 1873
Aged 84 yrs. & 5 mos.

Persecuted for
wearing the beard.

∽§ 173. PITTSFIELD, VT.:

> Jack York, died 1874, age about 85 yrs.
> He came to Pittsfield in 1820
> Born a Slave in Salem, N. Y.
> He was always ready to put his hand out
> in friendship to all.

∽§ 174. WEST RIPLEY, ME.:

> John L. Jones
> 1811-1875

> I came without my own consent,
> Lived a few years much discontent,
> At human errors grieving.
> I ruled myself by reason's laws,
> But got contempt and not applause
> Because of disbelieving.

> For nothing me could e'er convert
> To faith some people did assert
> Alone could gain salvation.
> But now the grass does me enclose
> The superstitious will suppose
> I'm doomed to Hell's damnation.

> But as to that they do not know;
> Opinions oft from ignorance flow,
> Devoid of some foundation.
> Tis easy men should be deceived
> When anything by them's believed
> Without a demonstration.

❧ 175. CHESTERFIELD, N.H.:

Roswell Stowell
who died Dec. 2, 1875
in his 60th year.

Let no one stand behind my grave,
 Now that I am called to rest,
Nor shed a tear that I am gone,
 For what I need is rest.

Rest from the weary load of care,
 Rest from the wearing pain:
For Death shall ever be to me
 An everlasting gain.

I know the road was bright and fair
 Or once it seemed to be.
But it has changed so much of late,
 It has few charms for me.

◄§ 176. GEORGE GREGORY, 1877, age 63, Guilford, Vt.
(—and he was a farmer, not a doctor):

> The first man in this country
> to promulgate the idea of
> female medical schools.

◄§ 177. MARY R. BIRCHARD, age 38, Newfane, Vt.:

> Died at Ashtabula, Ohio, Dec. 29, 1876. Her body
> was entirely consumed in the terrible Railroad Disaster
> which occurred at that place.
>
> But no man Knowest of her Sepulchre.

◄§ 178. ROXANNA ELWELL, 1876, age 16, Shaftsbury,
Vt.:

> She was young & gay & strong
> To Hail Mountain Grange she did belong;
> And the youngest of them all
> The first the Lord saw fit to call.

◄§ 179. LORENZO SABINE, 1877, age 74, Eastport, Me.:

> Transplanted.

◄§ 180. CAPT. AUGUSTUS N. LITTLEFIELD, 1878, age 75,
Newport, R.I.:

> An experienced and careful master
> mariner who never made a call upon
> underwriters for any loss.

181. REPORTED around 1880 as having stood in a Nantucket, Mass., graveyard (—and also in Searsport, Me., and Barre, Vt., for Solomon Pease):

> Under the sod and under the trees
> Lies the body of Jonathan Pease.
> He is not here, there's only the pod:
> Pease shelled out and went to God.

182. MRS. SARAH C. WHITNEY, 1880, age 66, West Dummerston, Vt.:

> She was an active participant in all
> Reformatory movements, and a firm beliver in
> Spirit Communication, which was a solace
> in her declining years.

183. ONE OF THE best examples in New England of the trend beginning in the later 19th century to express sentiments with elaborate monuments, rather than with epitaphs, is the Laurel Glen Mausoleum in Cuttingsville, Vt., ordered by John P. Bowman (1816-1891) and completed in 1880 in memory of his family.

Because nothing else indicates so well the attitude which prompted such memorials, here are excerpts from a pamphlet by the architect-designer, in which he described the edifice (see also the illustration):

Hid away in a charming glen among the Green Mountains of Vermont, in a little rural Cemetery, stands a Grecian Tomb, destined from the solidity of its construction, to endure till the ruthless hand of Time shall have reduced to viewless atoms the massive blocks of granite of which it is built; and in some future age, when all that is of life to-day has passed to silence and pathetic dust, and been forgotten, some hoary antiquarian will pause in silent contemplation at this mortuary pile, and wonder in what age 'twas built.

One year's time was absorbed in constructing this mag-
nificent Tomb . . . and all that a lavish expenditure of
money, skillful engineering, and patient, honest toil could
do, has been done, to render it as imperishable as any
structure ever built by human hands. . . .

The Catacombs are lined with marble and filled in front,
internally, with plates of polished French glass, and ex-
ternally, with polished marble fronts, paneled with Grecian angle border lines, within which the inscriptions
are engraved. . . . Bold and finely carved marble Corbels
project from the wainscotting, on which rest turned and
polished consoles of statuary marble, surmounted, one by
the bust of Mrs. Bowman, the other by that of the eldest
daughter, and between the two, in front of the Catacombs, a marble pedestal standing on the floor, charmingly
draped, bears the sitting figure of Little Addie, an infant
daughter, resting on a luxurious cushion, its dimpled arms
outstretched beseechingly towards its mother; while just
beyond the Arcade stands the bust of husband and father,
on a unique Grecian marble pedestal, apparently regarding with a look of happy content, this immaculate family
group. . . . Illumination in the evening time, and when
the massive granite door is closed during the day, is ob-
tained from six beautiful bronze candelabras . . . and the
flickering tapers seem to give them an unrest, and a motion as of life, that generates a sacred awe and holy rever-
ence for this hallowed place of undisturbed repose of
precious human dust.

The legend on the vaulted Lintel of the Catacombs, "A
couch of dreamless sleep," and that on front of the Arcade

Lintel, "Sacred to the memory of a sainted wife and daughters," cut in relief and flanked by flowing sculptured sprays of Ivy and Laurel, together with the statuary group, tell a brief but touching tale of this beautiful tomb.

In addition to the statuary of the interior, a life size full length statue of Mr. Bowman is posed outside, in the act of ascending the granite steps to the Portal, with a mantle depending in drapery form from the left arm, in the negligé of sorrow, the left hand grasping a wreath of immortels graced with a flowing band ribbon from the clasp, bearing the inscription "To my wife and children," the right hand extended towards the Portal, bearing a key. This statue is a marvel of art, and a truthful example of arrested motion, telling its own story of grief and blighted hopes. . . .

If there be one evidence more potent than all others of the deep, sublime devotion of the human heart to the untimely lost, of fires eternal that on fond memory's altar glow, it is the consecration of material, time and money to the building of these holiest of all holy shrines where bruised and bleeding human hearts may linger to inhale the sweet forgetfulness from angelic censers swung and gently burning. . . . Laurel Glen Mausoleum will stand for centuries to perpetuate the well rounded, honorable, successful life and name of its most noble founder.

DISLIKERS of epitaphs have, through the years—and with longer or shorter inscriptions stating their feelings—disclaimed the value of a parting message carved on gravestones.

◄§ 184. Determinedly anonymous is the sentiment in Hartford, Conn., 1882:

> Those who cared for him while living
> will know whose body is buried here.
> To others it does not matter.

◄§ 185. Even more explicit is the stone reported as in Stowe, Vt.:

> I was somebody.
> Who, is no business
> of yours.

◄§ 186. WINSTEAD, CONN.:

> Aaron S. Burbank
> 1818   1883
>
> Bury me not when I am dead
> Lay me not down in a dusty bed
> I could not bear the life down there
> With earth worms creeping through my hair.

◄§ 187. HARRY ROCKWELL, 1883, age 89, East Hampton, Conn.:

> Landsmen or sailors
> For a moment avast,
> Poor Jack's main topsail
> Is laid to the mast.
> The worms gnaw his timbers
> His vessel's a wreck,
> When the last whistle sounds
> He'll be up on deck.

◄§ 188. ABEL SILAS McMAHON, 1884, age 2 years, New Milford, Conn.:

> In a moment he fled;
> He ran to the cistern and raised the lid—
> His father looked in, then did behold
> His child lay dead and cold.

A DREAMLESS SLEEP
EMBLEM OF ETERNAL LIGHT

⏵§ 189. Mrs. Eunice Page, 1888, age 73, Plainfield, Vt.:

Five times five years I lived a virgin's life
Nine times five years I lived a virtuous wife;
Wearied of this mortal life, I rest.

⏵§ 190. From *Whittlin's*, published by the Vermont Folklore Society, as in Fairfax, Vt.:

O fatal gun, why was it he
That you should kill so dead?
Why didn't you go off just a little high
And fire above his head.

⏵§ 191. Francis Magranis, 1891, age 85, South Hadley, Mass.:

My shoes are made
My work is done;
Yes, dear friends,
I'm going home.
And where I've gone
And how I fare
There's nobody to know
And nobody to care.

☙ 192 & 193. IN BARNSTABLE, MASS., are stones attesting to the varied interests of husband and wife. Dr. Thomas W. Fossett (1894), age "over 80," cites his Scots-Irish ancestry and indicates his belief in the value of plant remedies in medicine:

> I have practiced on the eclectic system
> in Mass., Ohio and Mich. for over 50 years
> and have never lost that number of patients.

Emily Fossett, 1885, age 72:

> I conversed with the spirits of the dead for
> forty years, as with the living.

☙ 194. CONCORD, MASS.:

> Ephraim Wales Bull
> The originator of the Concord Grape
> Born in Boston March 4, 1806
> Died in Concord September 26, 1895
> He sowed, others reaped.

☙ 195. ONE OF THE GREATEST of modern evangelists and co-composer of the popular Moody and Sankey *Gospel Hymns*, whose stone is near his birthplace in East Northfield, Mass.:

> Dwight L. Moody
> Born February 5, 1837
> Died 1899 in the 62nd year of his age
> Just 10 days before the opening of
> the 20th Century

> He that doeth the will of God abideth forever.

~§ 196. MARLBORO, VT.:

> Williston Winchester
> Son of Antipas & Lois Winchester
> Born 1822   Died 1902
>
> He never married.
>
> "Uncle Wid"
> One of nature's noblemen, a quaint old
> fashioned, honest and reliable man.
> An ideal companion for men and boys.
> Delighted in hunting foxes and lining bees.

~§ 197. JOSEPH W. HOLDEN, 1900, age 83, East Otisfield, Me.:

> Prof. Holden
> the old Astronomer
> discovered that the Earth
> is flat and stationary
> and that the sun and moon
> do move.

◄§ 198. SHELDON, VT.:

> Unknown man shot in
> the Jennison & Gallup Co.'s store
> while in the act of burglarizing
> the safe Oct. 13, 1905.
> (Stone bought with money
> found on his person.)

◄§ 199, 200, 201 & 202. IN A ROW at the foot of the Dunklee monument in Vernon, Vt., are modern granite stones commemorating a husband and three wives— Nelson (1812-1894), Sarah C. (1819-1856), Martha H. (1830-1861) and Orsaline (1827-1906):

N. D.

> N ow here at last beneath this ground
> E ven husband and wives are found.
> L eaving loved sons and daughters five,
> S ecure by hope in Heaven to rise.
> O h there the wicked cease to molest,
> N ow the weary findeth sweet rest.

S. C. D.

> S ince O Lord my life Thou gavest
> A nd also hast taken away,
> R eturn and be my children's guide
> A nd be Thou my companion's stay.
> H ark my Savior's voice I hear!
> C ease, I go—my treasure's there.

M. H. F.

Also an Infant Son

M ust I record this trying scene
A gain in acrostic form?
R est, dread monster! Cause of sadness,
T hy welcome time seems not yet come.
H ere grave! Unfold thy bosom wide,
A dmit her infant by her side.

H ere thus we part yet hope to meet:
                    Where O Where?

O. K. S.

O h dear Mother thou hast left us,
R eal our loss we deeply feel.
S ee us, God, who hast bereft us
A nd can all our sorrows heal.
L et us hope we soon shall meet thee
I n that day when life is fled.
N ow we trust in heaven to greet thee,
E nter where no tears are shed.

✌§ 203. ONECO, CONN.:

1854 Alonzo P. Love 1908

Vote No License

✌§ 204. ON THE FOUR SIDES of the partly defaced monument of Gratis P. Spencer, designed and cut by Mr. Spencer before his death in 1908, age 83, in Lyndon Center, Vt.:

A Dreamless Sleep
Emblem of Eternal Rest

Science has never killed or persecuted a single
person for doubting or denying its teaching,
and most of these teachings have been true;
but religion has murdered millions for doubting
or denying her dogmas and most of these dogmas
have been false.

All stories about gods and devils,
of heavens and hells, as they do not
conform to nature, and are not
apparent to sense, should be rejected
without consideration.

Beyond the universe there is nothing
and within the universe the supernatural
does not and cannot exist.

Natural law is of universal application
and all truth is manifest to sense; of all
deceivers who have plagued mankind, none are
so deeply ruinous to human happiness as those
imposters who pretend to lead by a light
above nature.

The lips of the dead are closed forever.
There comes no voice from the tomb.
Christianity is responsible for having cast
the [fable] of eternal fire over almost every grave.

Man will go down into the grave and
all his thoughts will perish. The uneasy
conscience which in this remote corner
has for a brief space broken the contented
silence of the [grave] will be at rest.
Matter will [not change] it. If no longer imperishable
monuments and immortal deeds, death itself and
love stronger than death, will be as though
they have never been. Nor will anything that is,
be better or be worse for all the labor, genius,
[ability] and sufferings of man have strived
through countless generations to effect.

✍§ 205. GOSHEN, N.H.:

Phillip Row's son
Died Oct. 8, 1915. age three
By ardent spirits

✍§ 206 & 207. TWIN STONES, Brattleboro, Vt.:

Josie A.	Della S.
wife of	wife of
Caleb S. Wall	Caleb S. Wall
Died Mar. 3, 1906	Died July 29, 1913
AE. 52 yrs.	AE. 46 yrs. 2 ms. 13ds.

One precious to our hearts
　　　　　has gone,
The voice we love is still.
The place made vacant in
　　　　　our home,
Can never more be filled.

But some day if we may enter
early through the pearly
　　　　　portals wide
they will be the first to
　　　　　meet us
over on the other side.

✍§ 208. DUBLIN, N.H.:

Matti William Oja, son of
Herman Oja. Born Nov. 18, 1912
Killed by an automobile
September, 1, 1915

✍§ 209. HENRY CLAY BARNEY, 1915, age 82, Guilford,
Vt.:

My life's been hard
And all things show it;
I always thought so
And now I know it.

◆§ 210. PHINEAS G. WRIGHT, 1918, age 89, Putnam, Conn.:

Going, But Know Not Where

◆§ 211. EAST DERRY, N.H.:

Lizzie James
wife of
Edmund R. Angell
1849-1932

"I don't know how to die."

◆§ 212. ON A BOULDER, Pawtucket, R.I.:

William P. Rothwell M.D.
1866-[1939]

This is on me.

℞

213. McKinley, Me.:

Charles M. Gott
April 25, 1892   February 3, 1943

Lost in the North Atlantic
when his ship was torpedoed
on the way to Greenland.

Served overseas in the Medical Corps
in World War I

214. Hardwick, Vt.:

Marshall

	Willie	She
He	1872-1944	Always
Never	His wife	Did
Did.	Della Longe	Her
	1876-	Best.

ᵒᵍ§ 215. SPOFFORD, N.H.:

Luella Carpenter
1852   1949

William C. Lamare
1902   1955
A Friend

Lovely and pleasant in their lives
In their death they were not divided

INDEX

(Numbers refer to epitaphs)

INDEX